FOR THE OLDER BEGINNER

THEORY BOOK

ACCELERATED

PIANO
Adventures® *by Nancy and Randall Faber*

CONTENTS

UNIT 1

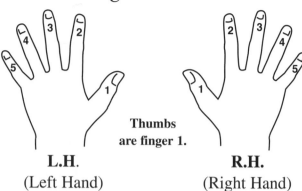

Finger Numbers

Thumbs are finger 1.

L.H.
(Left Hand)

R.H.
(Right Hand)

Finger Flashcards

- "Play" each flashcard *four times* on the closed keyboard lid.
  Saying the numbers aloud while playing will help you build finger coordination.

  Hint: Play with a rounded hand position on firm fingertips.

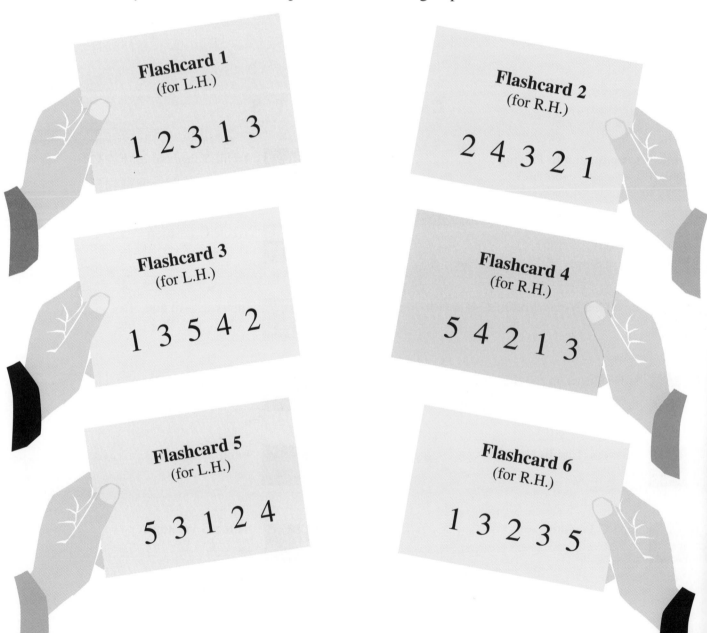

Flashcard 1
(for L.H.)

1 2 3 1 3

Flashcard 2
(for R.H.)

2 4 3 2 1

Flashcard 3
(for L.H.)

1 3 5 4 2

Flashcard 4
(for R.H.)

5 4 2 1 3

Flashcard 5
(for L.H.)

5 3 1 2 4

Flashcard 6
(for R.H.)

1 3 2 3 5

Extra Credit: "Play" each flashcard on the closed keyboard lid with the metronome
ticking at ♩ = 100.

Improvise with High and Low Sounds

Low  **High**

← **DOWN** ── ── **UP** →

going LOWER in pitch   *going HIGHER in pitch*

To *improvise* means to create music "on the spot."
The following activities will help you *improvise*
using high and low sounds.

Soft, Tinkling Bells

Directions

1. First, *listen* to the teacher duet part
   to feel the rhythm and the mood.

2. When you are ready, play any **black keys**
   HIGH on the piano. Create "soft bell
   sounds" going *higher* and *lower*.

3. As the duet fades, play *higher* and *higher*,
   gradually fading away.

> *piano* is the Italian word
> for soft.
>
> *p* is the abbreviation for *piano*.

Teacher Duet:

R.H.   Slowly

L.H.

Deep, Rich Gongs

Directions

1. First, *listen* to the teacher duet part
   to feel the rhythm and the mood.

2. When you are ready, play any **black keys**
   LOW on the piano. Create the sound of
   "deep, rich gongs" going *lower* and *higher*.

3. As the duet fades, end with a final
   forte gong on the lowest black key.

> *forte* (pronounced FOR-tay) is
> the Italian word for loud.
>
> *f* is the abbreviation for *forte*.

Teacher Duet:

R.H.   Moderately

L.H.

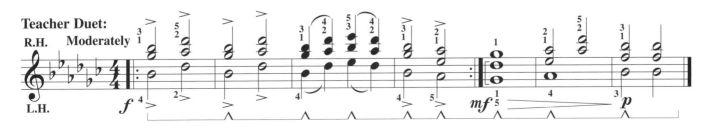

The Music Alphabet

The 7 letters of the music alphabet are repeated over and over up the keyboard.

Keyboard Map

1. **C**s are to the *left* of the two black keys.
   Label all the **C**s on the keyboard above.

2. **F**s are to the *left* of the three black keys.
   Label all the **F**s on the keyboard above.

3. Write **D** and **E** on the white keys
   between C and F on the keyboard above.

4. Write **G A B** on the white keys *between*
   F and C on the keyboard above.

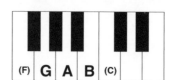

Spelling Bee

• Write the names of the keys marked. They spell words.

___ ___ ___ ___   ___ ___ ___

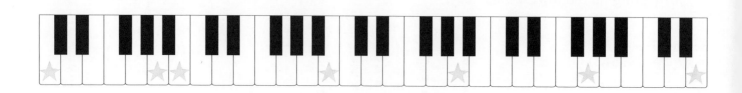

___   ___ ___   ___   ___   ___   ___

An **interval** is the distance between two keys.
From C to E is the interval of a **third (3rd)**.

3rds on the Keyboard

1. Name the key for each X going UP in **3rds**.
(Hint: It is helpful to silently say the key in between each X.)

Depress the **sustain (right-foot) pedal**. Then play and say the 3rds going HIGHER.

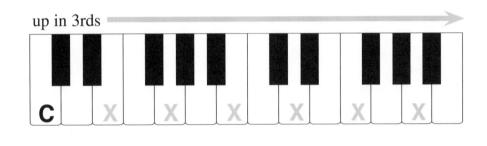

2. For notes *going down* the keyboard, learn the music alphabet going backwards.

Say: **G F E D C B A**

> Repeat until you
> have it memorised.

3. Name the key for each X going DOWN in **3rds**.
(Hint: Saying the music alphabet backwards will help you name the keys.)

Depress the **sustain pedal**. Then play and say the 3rds going LOWER.

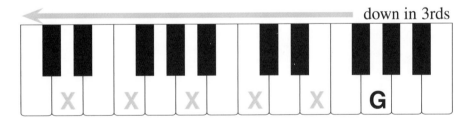

4. Write the letter name a 3rd UP or DOWN from each key marked.
Then play each example on the keyboard.

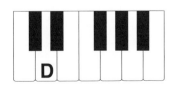

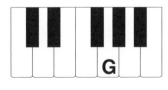

down a 3rd   *up* a 3rd   *up* a 3rd   *down* a 3rd

Lessons p.9

Rhythm Flags

1. Study the rhythm flag to the right.

Then complete the other flags by drawing **semibreves**, **minims** or **crotchets** above the counts.

crotchets (quarter notes) count "1"

minims (half notes) count "1 - 2"

semibreve (whole note) count "1 - 2 - 3 - 4"

Ex.

2. For each flag, choose any key and play the rhythm on the keyboard. (Play the notes from top to bottom.) **Count aloud, keeping a steady beat.**

Extra Credit: Can you tap your foot on each beat as you play and count? (Your teacher will demonstrate.)

The Bar

To organise rhythm, beats are grouped into *bars*.
Each bar has the same number of beats.

Bar lines divide the music into bars.

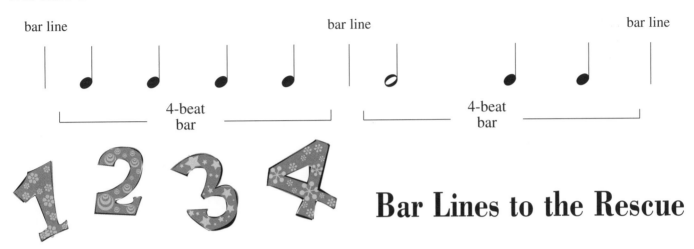

Bar Lines to the Rescue

Bar lines make it easier to read and feel the rhythm.

1. Organise the beats by drawing bar lines after every **4 beats**.

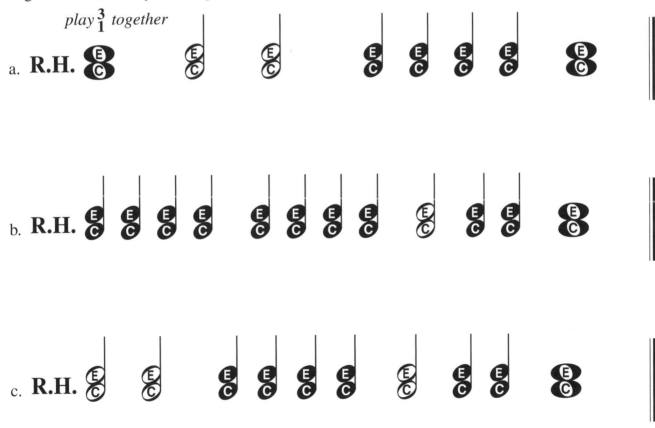

2. Now play each rhythm on the keyboard with your **R.H.**, while counting aloud.
Can you tap the beats in your lap with your **L.H.** as your **R.H. plays**?

3. Your teacher will play **rhythm a, b,** or **c**.
Point to the rhythm you hear.

Intervals: 2nds and 3rds

(For more information on 2nds and 3rds,
see the Lesson Book, pages 12–13.)

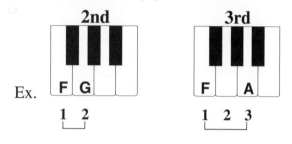

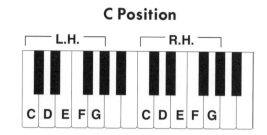

These **C Position melodies** use *2nds* and *3rds*.

1. Write 2nd or 3rd in the boxes for each interval.

Melody Inspection

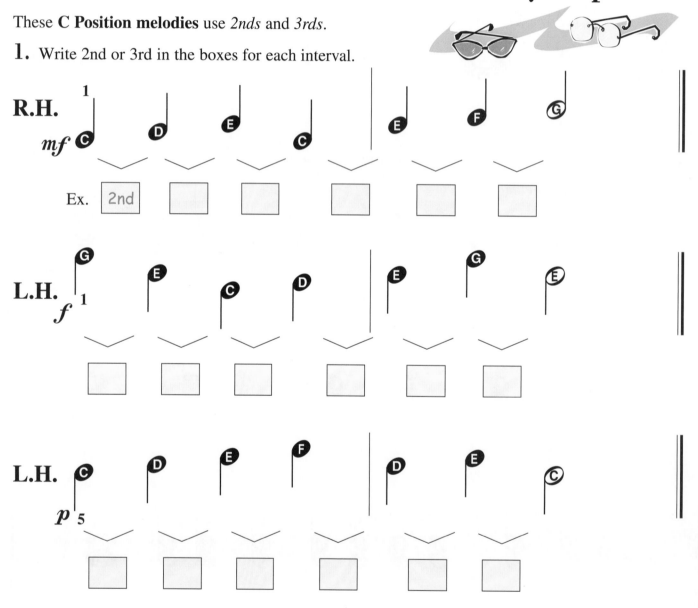

2. Play each **C Position melody** above on the keyboard.
   Say the letter names aloud as you play.

3. Improvise your own *2-bar* **C Position melody** that uses *2nds* and *3rds*.
   Play several with your right hand, then your left hand.

The word *sightreading* means to play through a piece without previous practice.

Hints for Success:

1. First notice the **2nds** (steps) and **3rds** (skips) in each melody.

2. Then sightread each melody s-l-o-w-l-y.

3. Keep your eyes on the music (not on your hands).

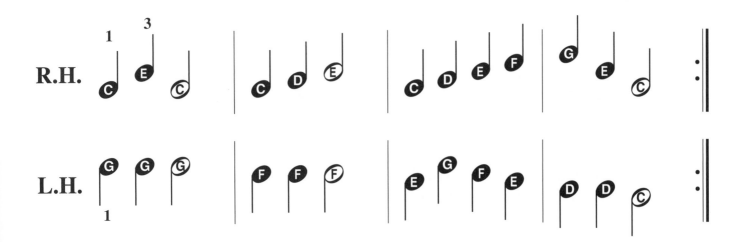

The examples below use *2nds* and *3rds*.

Your teacher will play example **a** or **b** on the piano.

Listen carefully and circle the example you hear.

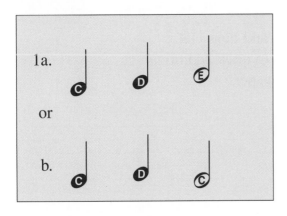

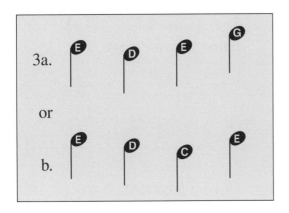

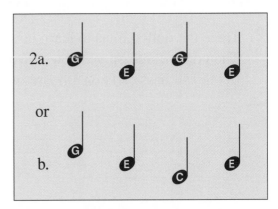

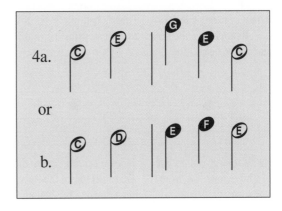

Lessons p. 13

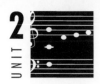

The Stave

The stave has 5 lines and 4 spaces.
Notes can be written *on the lines* or *in the spaces*.

5 Line Notes   **4 Space Notes**

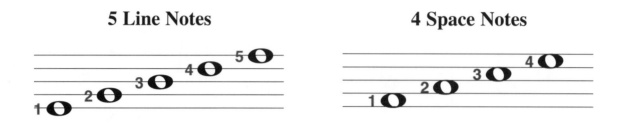

1. For each note on the stave below, write **L** for *line* note or **S** for *space* note.
   Then write the correct line or space number for each note.

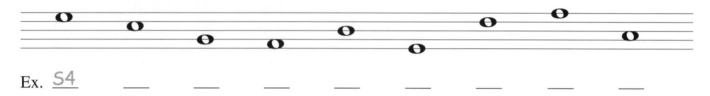

Ex. _S4_   ___   ___   ___   ___   ___   ___   ___   ___

Bass Clef and Treble Clef

2. Trace the dotted lines to learn how to draw the **treble clef** and **bass clef**.
   Then draw three on your own. (Your teacher may ask you to draw additional
   treble and bass clefs on a board or separate sheet of stave paper.)

start here ➝

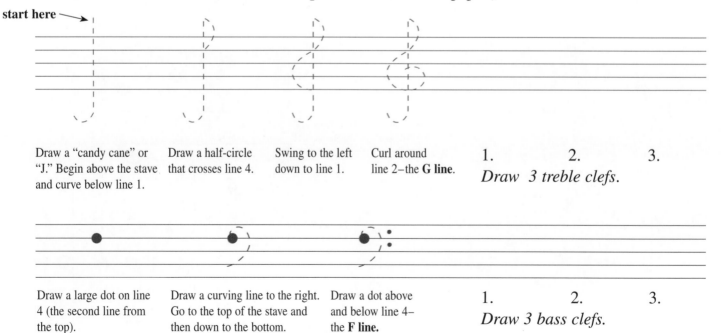

Draw a "candy cane" or "J." Begin above the stave and curve below line 1.

Draw a half-circle that crosses line 4.

Swing to the left down to line 1.

Curl around line 2–the **G line**.

1.   2.   3.
Draw 3 treble clefs.

Draw a large dot on line 4 (the second line from the top).

Draw a curving line to the right. Go to the top of the stave and then down to the bottom.

Draw a dot above and below line 4– the **F line.**

1.   2.   3.
Draw 3 bass clefs.

Time Signatures

$\frac{4}{4}$ = 4 beats in each bar ("1-2-3-4")
= The crotchet ♩ receives one beat.

$\frac{3}{4}$ = 3 beats in each bar ("1-2-3")
= The crotchet ♩ receives one beat.

Two-Hand Rhythms

In piano music, each hand may have its own rhythm.

1. Tap these exercises to increase your skill with rhythm.
   The **R.H.** taps the *top* line while the **L.H.** taps the *bottom* line.
   (Your teacher may demonstrate.)

Count aloud, "1-2-3-4." *Notice the accent on beat 1.*

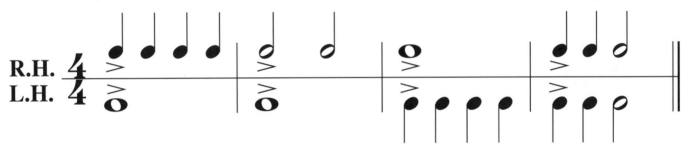

Count aloud, "1-2-3."

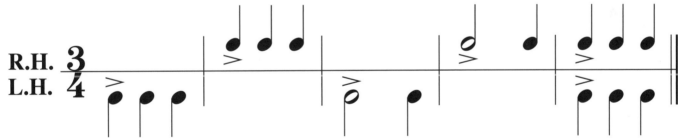

Count aloud, "1-2-3-4." *The arrows will guide your eyes.*

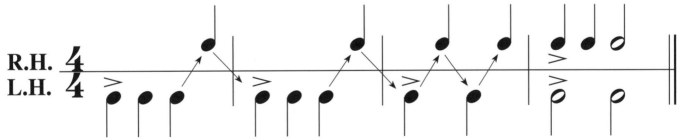

2. Your teacher may ask you to tap the rhythms above with the metronome.

   Slowly: ♩ = 60   Moderately: ♩ = 92   Quickly: ♩ = 120

Lessons p. 15

New Notes: Middle C and Treble Clef G

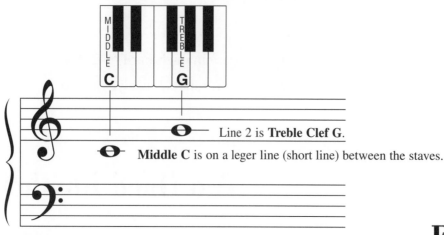

Line 2 is **Treble Clef G**.

Middle C is on a leger line (short line) between the staves.

First Composition

1. Draw **Middle C** or **Treble Clef G** for each bar below. Remember, each bar must have *4 beats*. You may follow the rhythm given above the stave as a guide.

2. Play s-l-o-w-l-y while your teacher plays Duet 1.
   Then play *quickly* while your teacher plays Duet 2.
   Listen to the difference in the mood!

FF

The Pedals of the Piano

The piano has two or three pedals.

If a grand piano is available, do the following:

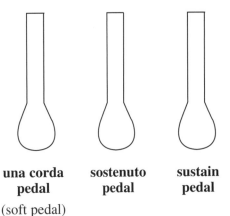

una corda
pedal
(soft pedal)

sostenuto
pedal

sustain
pedal

Sustain Pedal

1. Look inside the piano as you depress the sustain pedal. Notice the *dampers* (felts) are raised off the strings. This allows the strings to continue vibrating after the key is released. When you lift the sustain pedal, the dampers fall back onto the strings, stopping the sound.

2. Play a **low note** and depress the sustain pedal. Then play **high 3rds** with the R.H. *Listen* to the ringing sound created by the sustain pedal.

Una Corda Pedal (literally "one string")

Most piano keys have three strings which together produce one pitch. A hammer strikes all three strings to produce a full, rich tone. The lower range has only one or two strings per key.

3. Look inside a grand piano and watch the hammers as you depress the *una corda* pedal. Did you notice the keyboard and all the hammers shift to the right? Now the hammer will strike only two of the three strings, for a muted sound.

4. Play Middle C and Treble Clef G together **without** the *una corda* pedal. Now depress the *una corda* pedal and play these keys again. Did you hear a difference in the sound?

Sostenuto Pedal

(optional—not on all pianos)

The *sostenuto* pedal is useful for sustaining a low note (or notes) while both hands play high on the keyboard. (Use the left foot for the sostenuto pedal.)

5. Play a *low* note and depress the **sostenuto pedal**. Now play some high keys. Notice the crisp high sounds while only the bass continues to ring. Notes that are played *after* the sostenuto pedal is depressed will not be sustained.

6. Darken the appropriate pedal for each sound.

- •The musical passage is marked *pianissimo* (very soft).

- •The music requires a ringing, "blend" of sound.

- •You would like to hold a bass note while both hands play *staccato*.

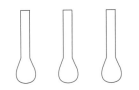

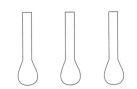

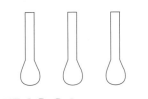

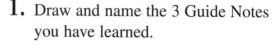

Three Guide Notes:

Bass Clef F, Middle C, and **Treble Clef G** will guide you as you learn new notes on the stave.

Treble Clef G (line 2)

Middle C

NEW: Bass Clef F
(4th line up or
2nd line down)

1. Draw and name the 3 Guide Notes you have learned.

 **Finding Guide Notes**

2. Draw a **bass clef**.
Then shade all the **Bass Clef Fs** on the stave.

3. Draw a **treble clef**.
Then shade all the **Treble Clef Gs** on the stave.

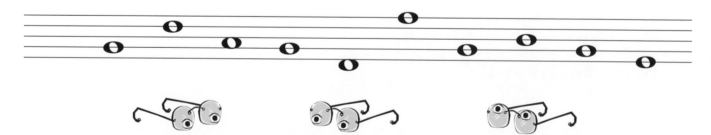

4. On the grand stave below, circle the three Guide Notes you have learned:
Middle C, Treble Clef G, and **Bass Clef F**.

14

2nds (Steps) on the Stave

On the stave, the interval of a **2nd** (step) is from:

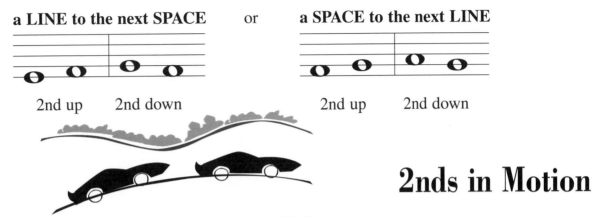

| a LINE to the next SPACE | or | a SPACE to the next LINE |

2nd up   2nd down   2nd up   2nd down

2nds in Motion

Remember, notes can move UP, move DOWN, or REPEAT.

1. Draw arrows below the noteheads to show the **up**, **down**, or **repeated** movement of the notes.

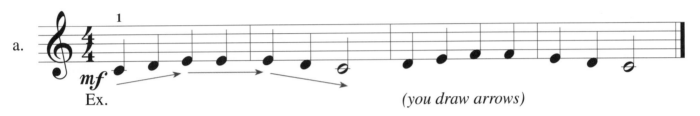

a.   *mf*
Ex.   *(you draw arrows)*

b.   *mf*

c.   *p*

d.   *mf*

2. Play each melody above s-l-o-w-l-y.

Watch for the **up**, **down**, or **repeated** movement of the notes.

3. Then write the **letter name** above each note.

Lessons p. 22

C Position Notes

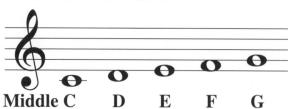

Middle C   **D**   **E**   **F**   **G**

Composing a Medieval Chant*

1. Compose your own chant using the **C Position notes** shown above.
   Use the rhythm given above each bar.

2. After completing your melody, draw **slurs** as shown.
   Remember, a slur means to play *legato*. (See Lesson Book, page 24 for review.)

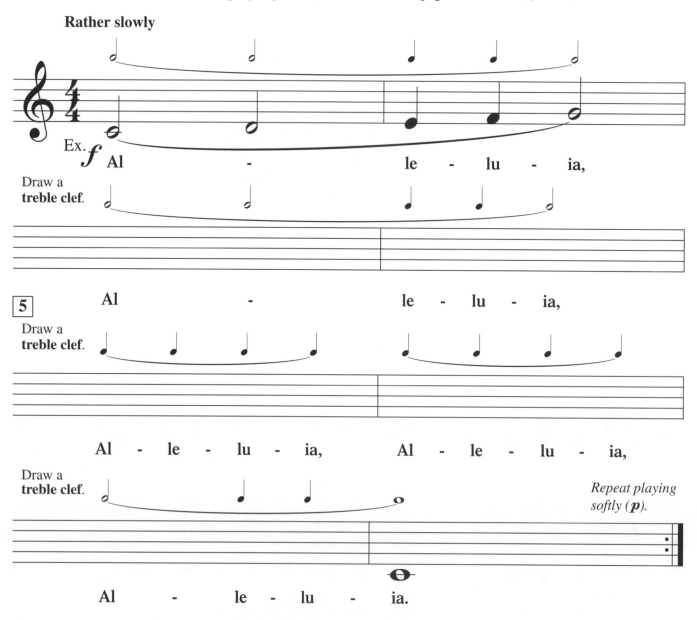

Rather slowly

Ex. *f* Al - le - lu - ia,

Draw a **treble clef**.

5 Al - le - lu - ia,

Draw a **treble clef**.

Al - le - lu - ia,   Al - le - lu - ia,

Draw a **treble clef**.

Repeat playing softly (p).

Al - le - lu - ia.

3. Now enjoy playing your chant. Listen for a smooth, *legato* sound.
   You may wish to play your chant **hands together**.
   (Your L.H. will play the same melody in a lower C Position.)

*Medieval—relating to the Middle Ages (AD 476–1453). The 1000 year period before the Renaissance.
 Chant—a simple, single-line melody for voices, sung rather freely.

For each musical example, circle the correct description:

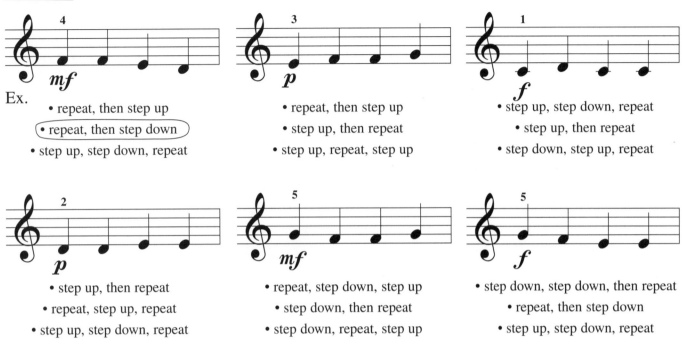

Ex.
- repeat, then step up
- (repeat, then step down)
- step up, step down, repeat

- repeat, then step up
- step up, then repeat
- step up, repeat, step up

- step up, step down, repeat
- step up, then repeat
- step down, step up, repeat

- step up, then repeat
- repeat, step up, repeat
- step up, step down, repeat

- repeat, step down, step up
- step down, then repeat
- step down, repeat, step up

- step down, step down, then repeat
- repeat, then step down
- step up, step down, repeat

Extra Credit: Play each example above on the keyboard.

Your teacher will play example **a** or **b**.
Listen carefully and circle the example you hear.

(Your teacher may ask you to play each example on the keyboard.)

New Note: Bass Clef G

Bass Clef G is a space note.
It is a 2nd (step) above **Bass Clef F**.
(Remember, Bass Clef F is a Guide Note.)

NEW
space note

O G

(Bass Clef F)

Guide Note Compass

1. Trace the bass clef *F line* on the stave below.
Then shade all the **Bass Clef Gs**.

2. Draw the *closest* Guide Note *to the left* of each note given.
Then name both notes in the blanks.

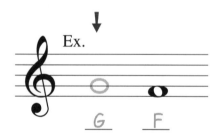

Ex.

G   F

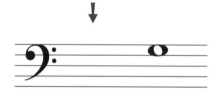

___ ___

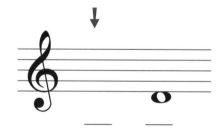

___ ___

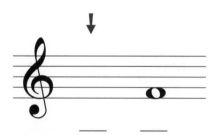

___ ___

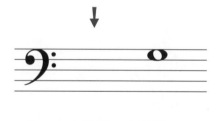

___ ___

Draw two Guide Notes.

higher G.N. ___ ___

lower G.N. ___

3. Draw a semibreve a **2nd above** or **below** the given note.
Then name both notes in the blanks.

___ ___

up a 2nd

___ ___

down a 2nd

___ ___

down a 2nd

___ ___

up a 2nd

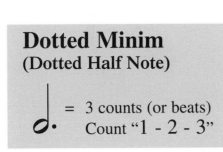

Dotted Minim
(Dotted Half Note)

= 3 counts (or beats)
Count "1 - 2 - 3"

Minuet Rhythms

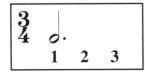

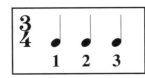

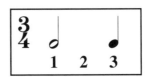

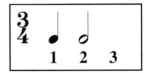

1. Complete the **rhythm** for this minuet by writing in your own rhythm for the blank bars. Choose from the ¾ rhythms shown above.

Then write the counts **1 - 2 - 3** under every bar.

(you write)

5

(you write)

2. Play your minuet rhythm on a *high G* with the teacher duet. Use R.H. finger 3.

Extra Credit: Can you play **hands together**?
(L.H. plays on a *lower G* with finger 3.)

Teacher Duet: (Student plays *high* on the keyboard)

Lessons p. 27

New Notes B and A

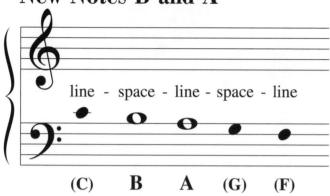

line - space - line - space - line

(C)   B   A   (G)   (F)

Theme from *Exsultate, Jubilate*

Mozart's Melody
(Study Piece)

Answer the Study Questions below to become more familiar
with one of Mozart's famous melodies for soprano and orchestra.

Wolfgang Amadeus Mozart
(1756–1791, Austria)

Moderately

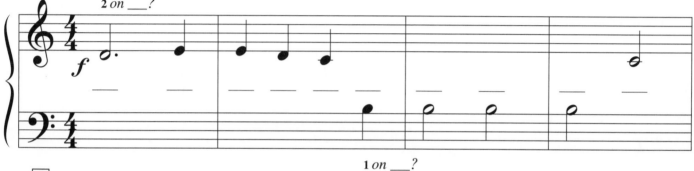

A Closer Look at Mozart's Melody

(Study Questions)

1. a. How many beats are in each bar? _____
   (fill in)
   b. Name each note in the blanks given.

   c. Circle all the repeated notes. (Hint: Be sure to look across the bar lines.)

   d. Which bar uses this rhythm? ♩. ♩ *bar* _____
   (fill in)
   e. Which bar uses this rhythm? ♩ ♩ ♩ *bar* _____
   (fill in)

2. Now play Mozart's melody. If a digital keyboard is available,
   play using the choir or chorus setting.

20

Remember, the word *sightreading* means to play through a piece without previous practice. Review the hints below. Then sightread these **left-hand melodies**.

Hints for Success:

1. Set a steady beat by counting one "free bar."

2. Focus your eyes on the noteheads (the round part).

3. Play rather slowly, always moving your eyes ahead.

Count one "free bar." ("1-2-3-4")

("1-2-3-4")

("1-2-3")

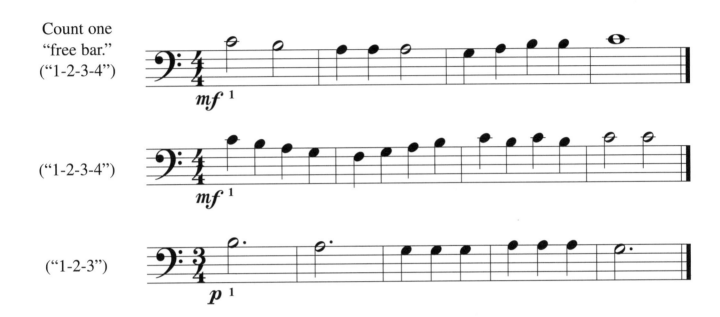

Listen as your teacher plays **rhythm a** or **b**.
Circle the rhythm you hear.
Then write the **time signature** in the box.

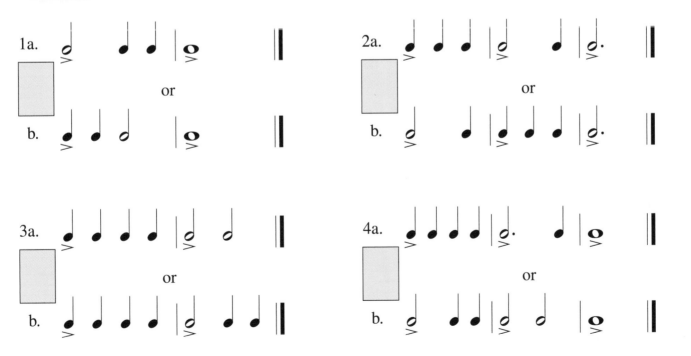

Extra Credit: Now you choose **rhythm a** or **b** and tap it for your teacher.
Your teacher will point to the rhythm heard.

3rds (Skips) on the Stave

On the stave, the interval of a **3rd (skip)** is from:

a LINE to the next LINE   or   **a SPACE to the next SPACE**

3rd up   3rd down   3rd up   3rd down

1. Write **2nd** or **3rd** for each interval.

Ex. 3rd

2. Draw the note a **2nd** or **3rd** from each Guide Note below.
Then name both notes in the blanks.

Ex.   *up* a 3rd
F   A

down a 2nd
___ ___

down a 3rd
___ ___

up a 2nd
___ ___

down a 3rd
___ ___

down a 2nd
___ ___

up a 2nd
___ ___

up a 3rd
___ ___

Extra Credit: Play each example on the keyboard. You choose the starting finger.

Improvise with Camptown Races

To improvise with *Camptown Races*:

Step 1. Play *bars 1-8* as written, with the teacher duet.

Step 2. Then move immediately **to the black keys** and improvise with the teacher duet.

Step 3. When you hear your teacher finish singing, *"Oh, doo-dah-day (2-3-4),"* return
immediately **to the white keys** and play *bars 1-8* to end.
Repeat as often as you like!

Stephen Foster
(1826–1864, U.S.A.)

Teacher Duet: (Student plays *1 octave higher*)

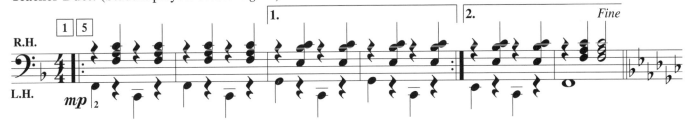

Step 2 Student *improvises* on the **black keys** with the teacher duet.
(The teacher may keep taking the 1st ending for a longer improvisation.)

Teacher Duet: (Student plays *high*)

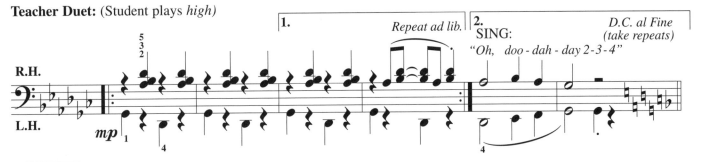

Step 3 When the teacher sings, *"Oh, doo-dah-day 2-3-4,"* immediately
repeat **Step 1** on the white keys.

Lessons p. 31

Crotchet Rest
(Quarter Rest) ♩

The crotchet rest = 1 beat of *silence*

Drawing the Crotchet Rest

1. Trace these 3 **crotchet rests**. Then draw 5 crotchet rests on your own.

　　　　　　1.　　　　2.　　　　3.　　　　4.　　　　5.

(you draw)

Eine Kleine Rock

2. Create a "rhythm piece" by writing your own 4/4 rhythm in each blank bar.
Use a crotchet rest in each bar you compose.

(you write)

(you write), etc.

3. Explore playing your rhythm piece **hands together**.
Play the two **lowest Cs** on the keyboard. (Use finger 3s.)
If a digital keyboard is available, play using a drum setting.

Repeat 2 times.
(2nd time 8*va*)
(3rd time 15*ma*)

Teacher Duet: (Student plays the *2 lowest Cs* on the keyboard.)

REVIEW: A **slur** curves over or under a group of notes. Connect these notes.

NEW: A **tie** connects one note to the very *same* note. Hold, and don't replay the tied note.

 Write **slur** or **tie** under each example below.
Your teacher may ask you to play each example.

_____ _____ _____

_____ _____ _____

 Your teacher will play a **2nd** or **3rd**.
Listen carefully and circle the interval you hear.

1.	2nd	2.	2nd	3.	2nd	4.	2nd	5.	2nd
	or		or		or		or		or
	3rd		3rd		3rd		3rd		3rd

For Teacher Use Only (The examples may be played in any order.)
Suggestion: Ask students to close their eyes as you play. You may wish to continue this eartraining, choosing more 2nds and 3rds. The student may answer verbally.

Quavers
Eighth (8th) Notes

 ← flag

A single quaver has a *flag*.

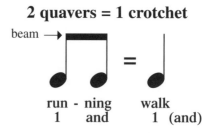

2 quavers = 1 crotchet

beam →

run - ning   walk
1   and   1   (and)

Two (or more) quavers are connected by a beam.

Rhythm Flags

1. Write the counts **1 + 2 + 3 + 4 +** (short for "1 and 2 and 3 and 4 and")
for each ₄⁴ rhythm flag. Note: Each beat is subdivided into two equal parts.

Write the counts **1 + 2 + 3 +** for each ₄³ rhythm flag.

Ex. 1 + 2 + 3 + 4 +

(you write the counts)

(you write the counts)

(you write the counts)

2. Now clap or tap each "flag," counting aloud.

The Phrase

A *phrase* is a musical idea or thought.
A phrase is often shown in the music
by a slur, also called a *phrase mark*.

This Train

This piece is composed of five **phrases**.

- Trace the opening *phrase mark* to show the first phrase.
- Then draw the four additional phrase marks to complete the piece.

Brightly

Traditional Spiritual

Check yourself. Do you have *five* phrase marks in this piece?

- Now play *This Train*. Listen for the beginning and end of each phrase.

Lessons p. 38

Anacrusis (or Upbeats)

The note or notes in an incomplete opening bar are called *anacrusis* or *upbeat(s)*.
An anacrusis leads into the first full bar.

If a piece begins with an anacrusis, the last bar is often incomplete. The combined beats of the first and last bars will equal one full bar.

The Ash Grove
(Study Piece)

English folk song

Answer the Study Questions below to become more familiar with this English folk song.

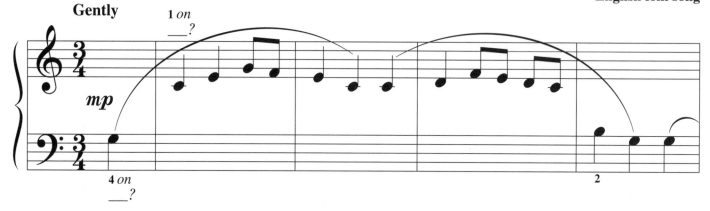

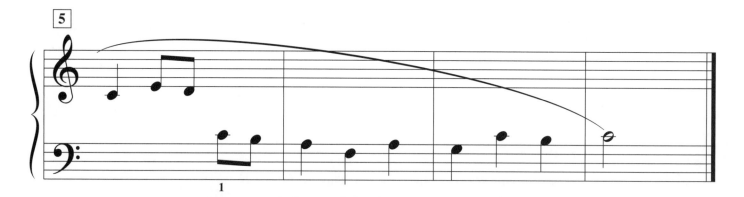

A Closer Look at The Ash Grove

(Study Questions)

1. a. Does this piece begin on *beat 1, 2,* or *3*? ___

   b. Write the counts **1 + 2 + 3 +** for each bar.

   c. How many phrases (musical sentences) are in this piece? ___

   d. Name the *lowest* note in the piece. ___ Name the *highest* note. ___

2. Now play *The Ash Grove*.
If a digital keyboard is available, play using the guitar setting.

Each example has one or more **upbeats**.
Answer each question, and then sightread the music.

Begins on beat ___?

The Riddle Song
(American folk song)

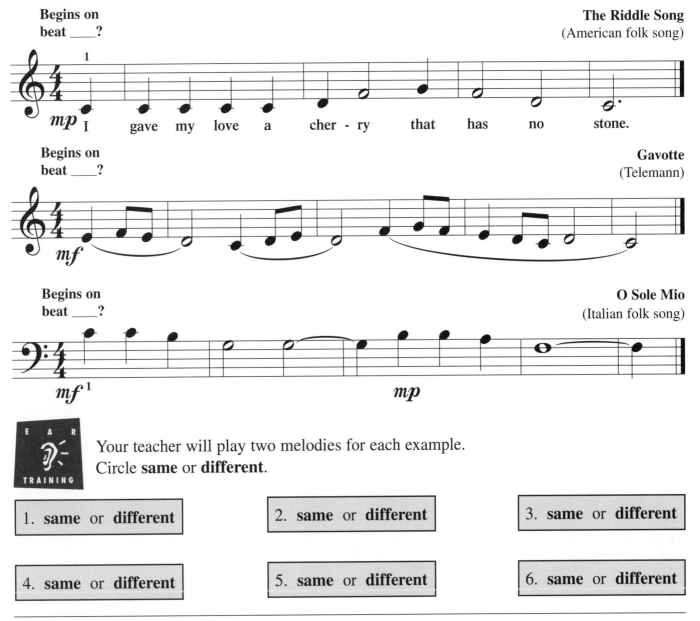

I   gave   my   love   a   cher - ry   that   has   no   stone.

Begins on beat ___?

Gavotte
(Telemann)

Begins on beat ___?

O Sole Mio
(Italian folk song)

Your teacher will play two melodies for each example.
Circle **same** or **different**.

1. **same** or **different**   2. **same** or **different**   3. **same** or **different**

4. **same** or **different**   5. **same** or **different**   6. **same** or **different**

For Teacher Use Only: (The examples may be played in any order.)
Suggestion: Ask students to close their eyes as you play.

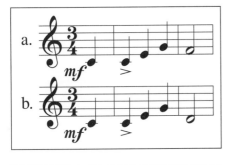

Lessons p. 40

New Guide Note: Bass C

Guide Notes serve as "anchor notes" for reading other notes on the stave.

Guide Note Bass C is space 2 in the bass clef. (Spaces are numbered from bottom to top.)

4 Guide Notes

Treble Clef G
Middle C

Bass Clef F
NEW: Bass C

● Name each Guide Note in the blanks given.
  Then play *Guide Note Blues* with the teacher duet.

Guide Note Blues

Teacher Duet: (Student plays *as written*)

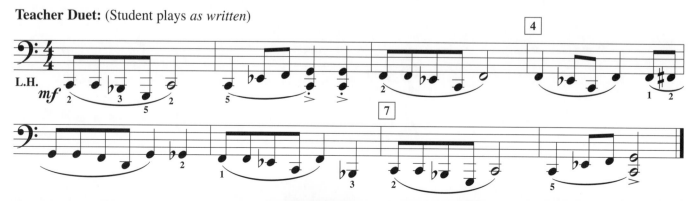

Reading in Bass C Position

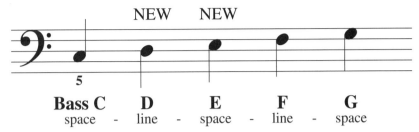

NEW NEW

Bass C   **D**   **E**   **F**   **G**
space - line - space - line - space

Guide Note Strategy

Guide Notes can help you quickly name other notes on the grand stave.

- Draw the *closest* Guide Note *to the left* of each note given.
- Then name both notes in the blank.

Draw 2 Guide Notes

Ex. __C__ __D__
closest
Guide Note

___ ___
closest
Guide Note

___ ___ ___ ___
closest
Guide Notes

Draw 2 Guide Notes

___ ___
closest
Guide Note

___ ___
closest
Guide Note

___ ___
closest
Guide Notes

___ ___
closest
Guide Note

___ ___
closest
Guide Note

___ ___
closest
Guide Note

Lessons p. 43

A **theme** is a melody.
A theme can have several phrases.

Beethoven's Theme
C Position

1. **Play the first phrase of "Beethoven's Theme."**

> Notice that the first phrase sounds *incomplete*—like a musical question.
> It ends on a note *other* than C. C is the "key note" or "home note" in C Position.

2. **Now play the second phrase of "Beethoven's Theme."**

> Did you hear how the second phrase sounds *complete*, like a musical answer?
> It has a final, satisfying sound because it **ends on C**, the "key note" in C Position.
>
> • Is the rhythm of the *first* phrase the same as the rhythm of the *second* phrase? _____

3. **Now play the third phrase of "Beethoven's Theme."**

> Notice how the rhythm of the third phrase becomes more active with quavers.
>
> • Does the third phrase end on C, the "key note"? _____
> • Does it sound like a musical *question* or *answer*? _____

4. **Now play the fourth phrase of "Beethoven's Theme."**

> • The fourth phrase is the same as which other phrase? _____
> • Does the fourth phrase sound like a musical *question* or *answer*? _____

Composing a Theme in C Position

Now that you have studied Beethoven's theme, write your own theme based on his great masterpiece.

Bass C   D   E   F   G

1. Using the notes of the Bass C Position, compose your *first phrase* using Beethoven's rhythm.
   To compose a musical question, end on any note in C Position except C.

mf

2. Begin your *second phrase* with the same notes as the first phrase.
   To compose a musical answer, end on C (the "key note").

mf

3. Compose your *third phrase* in the treble clef. Use these notes: Middle C, D, E, F, G.
   To compose a musical question, end on any note in C Position except C.

p   *grow louder*

4. Complete your *fourth phrase* by simply **repeating your second phrase**—just as Beethoven did.

f

5. Enjoy playing your theme!
   If a digital keyboard is available, explore using the string setting.

Lessons p. 44

Staccato means a crisp, detached sound.

To play staccato, quickly bring the finger off the key.

The staccato mark is a small dot placed above or below the notehead.

Theme from the

"Staccato" Symphony

1. Write a *staccato* mark above or below each **crotchet notehead**.
Then play. *Listen* for a crisp, detached sound.

2. Trace the **slurs** marked below. Then play.
Listen for a smooth, connected sound.

Theme from the

"Legato" Symphony

34

For *staccato* notes, the dot is placed **above** or **below** the notehead.

For dotted minims, the dot is placed **beside** the notehead.

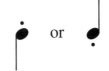 or

 or

● Circle each *staccato* note. Then name every note in the blank.

● Circle each *dotted minim*. Then name every note in the blank.

Your teacher will play six examples.
Write **S** for *staccato* or **L** for *legato*.
Write **SL** if you hear **both** *staccato* and *legato* sounds.

1. _____

2. _____

3. _____

4. _____

5. _____

6. _____

For Teacher Use Only: (The examples may be played in any order.)
Suggestion: Ask students to close their eyes as you play.

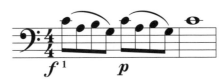

Treble Spaces: F A C E

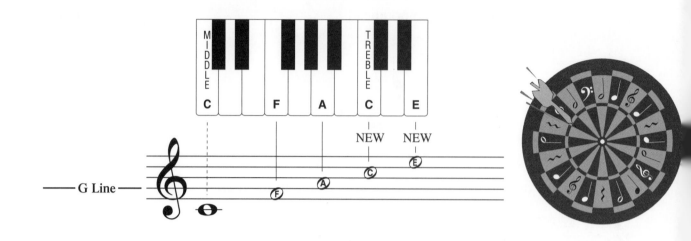

G Line

- Draw a line matching the note on each stave to the correct key on the keyboard.

Bull's-eye Notes!

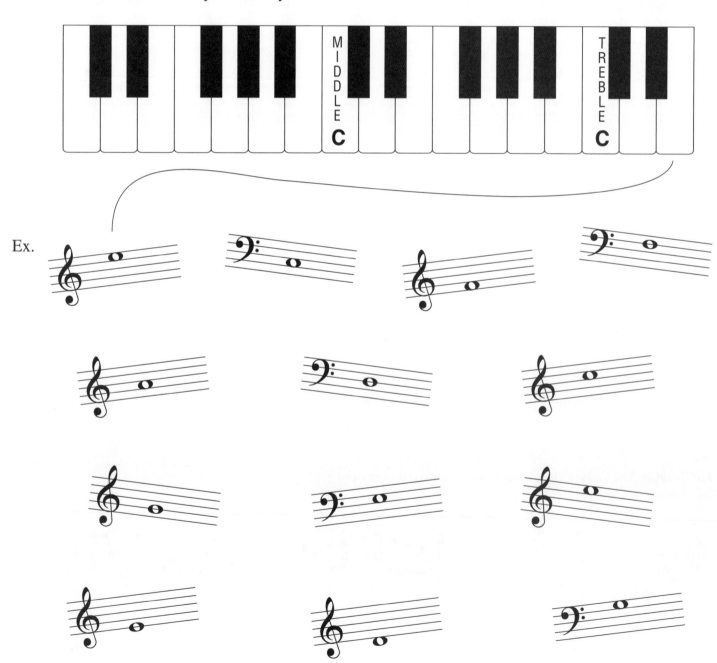

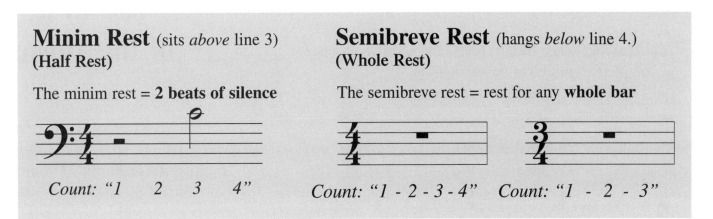

Minim Rest (sits *above* line 3)
(Half Rest)

The minim rest = **2 beats of silence**

Count: "1   2   3   4"

Semibreve Rest (hangs *below* line 4.)
(Whole Rest)

The semibreve rest = rest for any **whole bar**

Count: "1 - 2 - 3 - 4"   Count: "1 - 2 - 3"

I've Got Rhythm!

1. Write four bars of your own 4/4 rhythm.

Use at least one **minim rest**. (‐) Remember, each bar must have 4 beats.

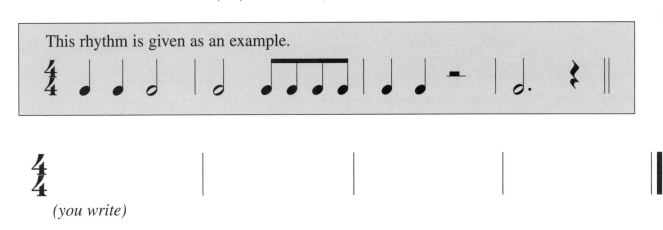

This rhythm is given as an example.

4/4

(you write)

2. Write four bars of your own 3/4 rhythm.

Use at least one **semibreve rest**. (‐)

3/4

(you write)

3. Write four bars of your own 4/4 rhythm.

Use at least **one crotchet rest (𝄽)**, **one minim rest**, and **one semibreve rest**.

4/4

(you write)

Lessons p. 52

37

The Rest of the Music

- Add **crotchet rests**, **minim rests**, and **semibreve rests** to complete each line of music below.

  (See page 37 of this book for a review of semibreve and minim rests.)

- Then play each musical example.

(See page 37 of this book for a review of semibreve and minim rests.)

"Fantasy-Impromptu" Theme
Frédéric Chopin

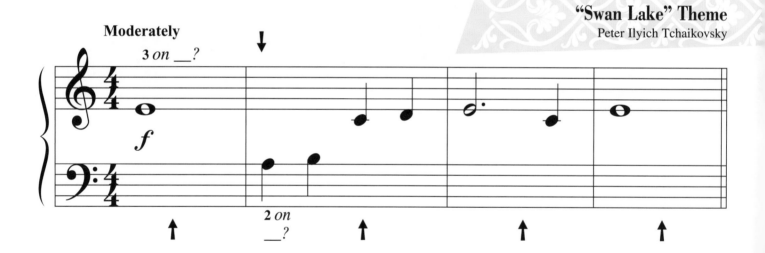

"Swan Lake" Theme
Peter Ilyich Tchaikovsky

Reminder: A semibreve rest is also used in ¾ for any whole bar.

"On Wings of Song" Theme
Felix Mendelssohn

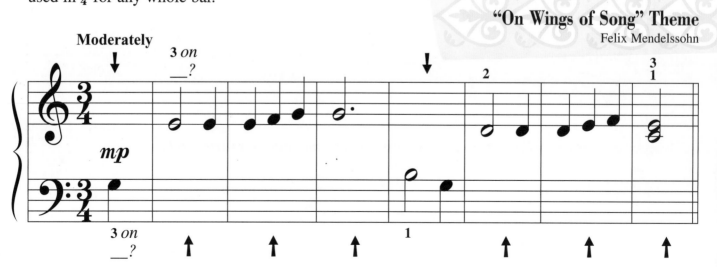

Identify each rest by writing **C** for crotchet rest, **M** for minim rest, or **S** for semibreve rest in each blank.

Put an X through the bars with **too many beats**.

Put an X through the bars with **too few beats**.

 Your teacher will set a steady beat for you to tap with your hand or foot.
As you tap, *listen* to the musical example that your teacher plays.
Circle the kind of rest you hear in each example.

1. 𝄽 (crotchet)   **2.** 𝄽 (crotchet)   **3.** 𝄽 (crotchet)

▬ (minim)   ▬ (minim)   ▬ (minim)

▬ (semibreve)   ▬ (semibreve)   ▬ (semibreve)

For Teacher Use Only: (The examples may be played in any order.)

Suggestion: Set a steady beat for the student to tap as you play.
Count one bar aloud before playing each example.

Lessons p. 52

6

Five Guide Notes

Using Guide Notes, you can find and name
other notes on the grand stave.

- Name each of these Guide Notes in the box.
  (For review, see Lesson Book, p.54)

- Draw the 5 Guide Notes you have
  learned on the grand stave below.

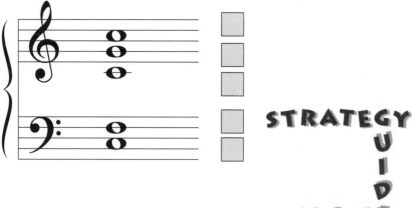

Guide Note Strategy

1. Draw the *closest* Guide Note *to the left* of each note given.
   Then name both notes in the blanks.

____ ____

closest
Guide Note

____ ____

closest
Guide Note

____ ____

closest
Guide Note

____ ____

closest
Guide Note

____ ____

closest
Guide Note

____ ____

closest
Guide Note

2. Play each example above on the keyboard.

Reading in Treble C Position

- Review these notes that step up
  from **Treble C**.

Treble C   D   E   F   G
space - line - space - line - space

- Draw the notes of the **Treble C Position**.

- Name each note for *Gavotte* in the blank below.

- Then play Telemann's melody. (Hint: Watch for
  2nds and **3rds**, as well as reading the note names.)

Gavotte*

**Georg Philipp Telemann
(1681–1767, Germany)**
adapted

*A *gavotte* is a lively French dance in $\frac{4}{4}$ time. It usually begins with upbeats on beats 3 and 4.

Carefree Day

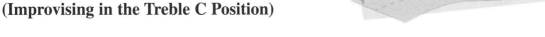

(Improvising in the Treble C Position)

1. *Listen* to your teacher play the duet. Feel the rhythm and the mood.

2. When you are ready, play any of the notes of the **Treble C Position**
   in *any* order. (Hint: Play repeated notes, long or short notes,
   loud and soft notes, etc.)

3. End by playing softer and softer with your teacher.

Teacher Duet: (for improvisation)

Lessons p. 55

Rules for Stems:

Notes **below line 3** have UP stems
on the *right* side of the notehead.

Notes **on or above line 3** have DOWN stems
on the *left* side of the notehead.

Famous Composers

- Draw stems correctly on the notes below.
- Then name the notes to spell the names of famous composers.

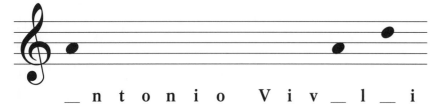

_ n t o n i o   V i v _ l _ i

Antonio Vivaldi (1678–1741)
Composer of *The Four Seasons*. Violinist
and composer who taught music at an
all-girl orphanage.

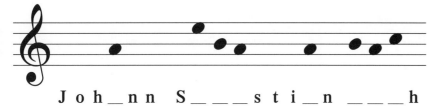

J o h _ n n   S _ _ _ s t i _ n   _ _ _ h

Johann Sebastian Bach (1685–1750)
Composer of the *Brandenburg Concertos*
and many keyboard works. Virtuoso
organist who served as director of several
great churches.

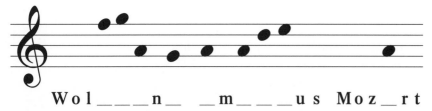

W o l _ _ _ _ n _   _ m _ _ _ _ u s   M o z _ r t

Wolfgang Amadeus Mozart (1756–1791)
Composer of *Don Giovanni* and *The Magic
Flute*. Child prodigy from Salzburg.
Composer to the Emperor of Austria.

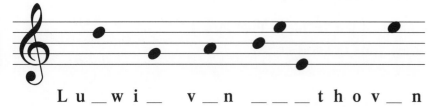

L u _ w i _   v _ n   _ _ _ t h o v _ n

Ludwig van Beethoven (1770–1827)
Composer of 9 symphonies and 32 piano
sonatas. Virtuoso pianist and conductor.
Deafness overcame him as he composed
his later works.

P _ t _ r   I l y i _ h   T _ h _ i k o v s k y

Peter Ilyich Tchaikovsky (1840–1893)
Composer of *The Nutcracker*. Russian
composer, pianist, and conductor.

Imitation is the immediate repetition of a musical idea played by the other hand.
Watch for **imitation** between the bass and treble clefs as you sightread these examples.
(Remember to set a steady beat of one full bar before beginning to play.)

Which hand is imitating? ____

Which hand is imitating? ____

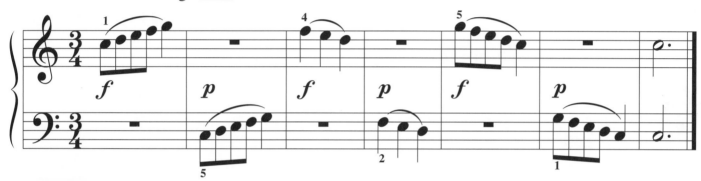

Your teacher will play two short musical phrases, one with each hand.
Circle **imitation** if the second phrase exactly *imitates* the first phrase.
Circle **no imitation** if the second phrase is *different* than the first one played.

1. **imitation** or **no imitation**	2. **imitation** or **no imitation**	3. **imitation** or **no imitation**
4. **imitation** or **no imitation**	5. **imitation** or **no imitation**	6. **imitation** or **no imitation**

For Teacher Use Only: (The examples may be played in any order.)
Suggestion: Ask students to close their eyes as you play.

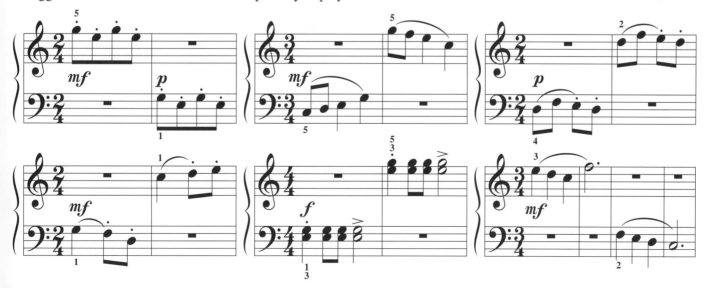

Lessons p. 58

The Interval of a Fourth (4th)

(For more review, see the Lesson Book, pages 60–61.)

A **4th** spans 4 letter names. Think:
    line *skip-a-line* **to a space** or
    space *skip-a-space* **to a line.**

To draw a **4th**, count the starting note and *each line* and *space*, including the last note.

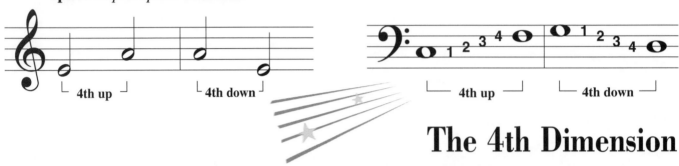

The 4th Dimension

1. Draw the note a **4th up** from each Guide Note. Then name both notes.

2. Draw the note a **4th down** from each Guide Note. Then name both notes.

3. Identify each interval as a **2nd**, **3rd**, or **4th** in the box above the stave. Then name both notes in the blanks given.

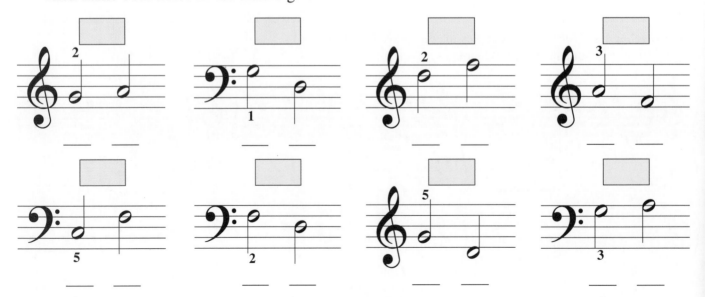

Extra Credit: Play each interval on this page for your teacher.

Write letter names **going up in 4ths** from the marked key. Then play them.

Write letter names **going down in 4ths** from the marked key. Then play them.

The interval of a **4th** appears five times in *each* line of music. Circle each **4th**. Then sightread the melodies.

Hint: A **4th** sounds like the opening of *Here Comes the Bride*. (Your teacher may sing it for you.)

Your teacher will play a **2nd**, **3rd** or **4th**. *Listen* carefully and circle the interval you hear. (You may wish to hum the interval first.)

1.	**2.**	**3.**	**4.**	**5.**
2nd	2nd	2nd	2nd	2nd
3rd	3rd	3rd	3rd	3rd
4th	4th	4th	4th	4th

For Teacher Use Only: (The examples may be played in any order.)
Suggestion: Ask students to close their eyes as you play.
The student will benefit from continued ear training with 2nds, 3rds, and 4ths.
The teacher may randomly choose intervals, with the student identifying each verbally.

Lessons p. 62

The Interval of a Fifth (5th)

(For more review, see the Lesson Book, pages 60 and 64.)

A 5th spans 5 letter names. Think:
line *skip-a-line* **to a line** or
space *skip-a-space* **to a space**.

To draw a **5th**, count the starting note and
each line and *space*, including the last note.

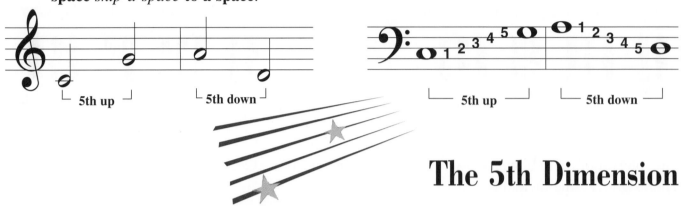

The 5th Dimension

1. Draw the note a **5th up** from each note given. Then name both notes.

2. Draw the note a **5th down** from each note given. Then name both notes.

3. Draw stems correctly on the notes below. (For review, see page 42.)
Identify each interval as a **2nd**, **3rd**, **4th** or **5th** in the box above the stave.

Extra Credit: Play each interval on this page for your teacher.
(Choose your own fingering.)

Write letter names **going up in 5ths** from the marked key. Then play them.

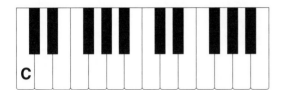

Write letter names **going down in 5ths** from the marked key. Then play them.

The interval of a **5th** appears three times in *each* line of music. Circle each **5th**. Then sightread the melodies.

NEW: A **5th** sounds like the opening of *Twinkle, Twinkle Little Star*.
REVIEW: A **4th** sounds like the opening of *Here Comes the Bride*.

Your teacher will play a **2nd**, **3rd**, **4th**, or **5th**. *Listen* carefully and circle the interval you hear. (You may wish to hum the interval first.)

1.	**2.**	**3.**	**4.**	**5.**
2nd	2nd	2nd	2nd	2nd
3rd	3rd	3rd	3rd	3rd
4th	4th	4th	4th	4th
5th	5th	5th	5th	5th

Lessons p. 65

Musical Form

The overall structure of a piece is called *musical form*.

This piece has three sections: an **A section**, **B section**, and the return of the **A section**. It is in **A B A form**.

A **barcarolle** is a piece imitating the rocking rhythm of a gondola (paddled boat).

First sightread this piece without the teacher duet. Then answer the Study Questions on the next page.

Barcarolle
(Study Piece)

Jacques Offenbach
(1819–1880, France)
arranged

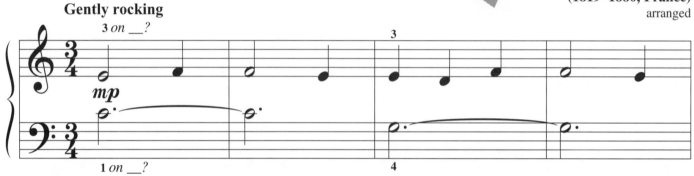

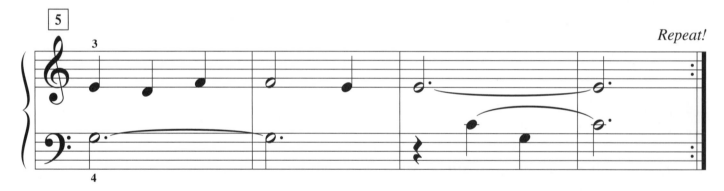

Teacher Duet: (Student plays *1 octave higher*)

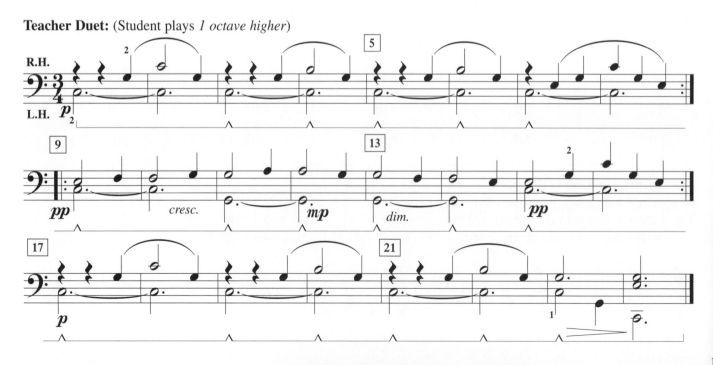

Repeat from bar 9.

A Closer Look at Barcarolle

(Study Questions)

1. a. Label the **A section**, **B section**, and the return of the **A section** in this piece.

   b. Circle two ways the **B section** is different from the **A section**.
      • R.H. melody   • L.H. melody   • different notes   • different length

   c. Draw semibreve rests to complete the **B section**.

   d. Write the counts **1 2 3** under the correct beats in the **A section**.

2. Now sightread *Barcarolle* again, with your teacher playing the duet.

The Sharp ♯

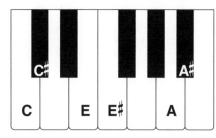

A sharp means to play the key that is a semitone HIGHER.

(For a review of semitones, see the Lesson Book, page 68.)

Looking Sharp!

1. Trace this **sharp.**
(two straight vertical lines, two slanted horizontal lines)

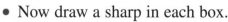

• Now draw a sharp in each box.

2. A sharp can be written on any line or in any space of the stave.

• Draw a sharp on each of the 5 lines of the stave. Notice the line passes through the *middle* of the sharp.

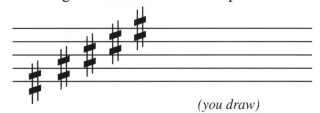

(you draw)

• Draw a sharp in each of the 4 spaces of the stave. Notice the "box" of the sharp fits inside the space.

(you draw)

3. A sharp carries through an entire bar, but not past a bar line.

• How many notes are played as G♯?_____

• How many notes are played as C♯?_____

• How many notes are played as F♯?_____

4. On the stave, a sharp sign is always placed *before* the note.
Draw a sharp *to the left* of each note below. Then name each note in the blank.

Ex. _A♯_

_____

_____

_____

_____

The Flat ♭

A flat means to play the key that is a semitone LOWER.

(For a review of flats, see the Lesson Book, page 72.)

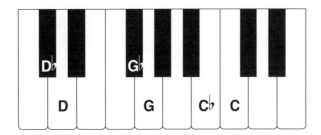

In Nothing Flat

1. Trace this **flat**.

• Now draw a flat in each box.

2. Circle the correct **flat keys** or **sharp keys** on the keyboard below.

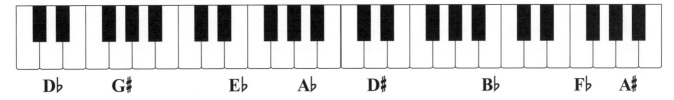

D♭   G♯   E♭   A♭   D♯   B♭   F♭   A♯

3. Write the **sharp name** and the **flat name** for each key with an X.

Ex. _C♯_ or _D♭_   ___ or ___   ___ or ___   ___ or ___   ___ or ___

4. A flat can be written on any line or in any space of the stave.

Draw flats for each line and space.

(you draw)   *(you draw)*

5. On the stave, a flat sign is always placed *before* the note.

Draw a flat *to the left* of each note below. Then name each note in the blank.

Lessons p. 72

51

The Natural ♮

A **natural** cancels a sharp or a flat.
A natural is always a white key.

(For a review of the natural, see the
Lesson Book, page 74.)

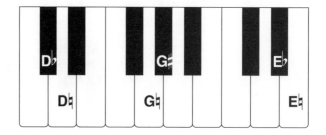

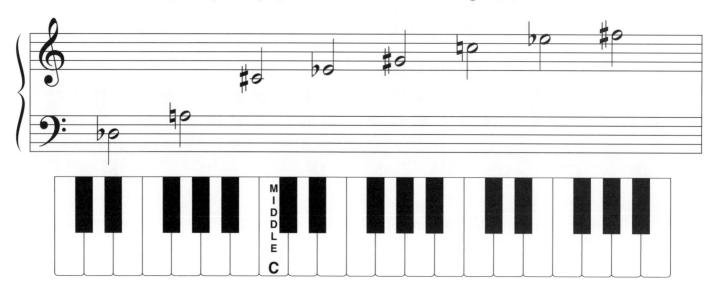

It's Just Natural

1. Draw a line from each note on the stave to the **correct key** on the keyboard.
(Your teacher may ask you to play each of these notes on the piano.)

2. A natural can be written on a line or in a space.

- Trace these naturals that are on a line.
  Then draw 3 of your own.
  Hint: Draw an "L", then a "7".

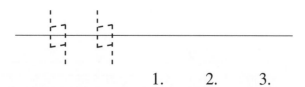

1.   2.   3.

- Trace these naturals that are in a *space*.
  Then draw 3 of your own.

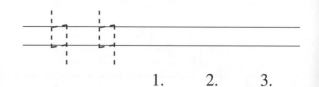

1.   2.   3.

3. There are two sharped notes per bar for *bars 1–3*. Make each bar
have only *one sharp* by adding a **natural**. Then sightread the melody.

Scan each melody below, noticing the **sharps**, **flats**, and **naturals**.
Then sightread at a slow tempo.
Remember to set a steady beat of one full bar before you begin playing.

 Your teacher will play example **a** or **b**.
Listen carefully and circle the example you hear.

Extra Credit: Your teacher may ask you to sightread each example.

Lessons p. 74

Tonic and Dominant

In the C Pentascale:

The **1st** scale degree is called the **tonic**.
The **5th** scale degree is called the **dominant**.

C Pentascale

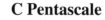

Scale degree: 1   2   3   4   5

↑ tonic   ↑ dominant

You're the Arranger!

1. Write the **tonic** or **dominant** note in the bass clef for each bar.
Here are hints to guide you:
- If the R.H. is mostly scale degrees 1 - 3 - 5, use the **tonic** note in the bass.
- If the R.H. is mostly scale degrees 2 - 4 - 5, use the **dominant** note in the bass.

Ode to Joy

Ludwig van Beethoven

Moderately

3 *on* __?

mf

Ex. **5**   *(you write)*

In May

Brightly

Ferdinand Beyer

5 *on* __?

mf   *p*

Ex. **5**   *(you write)*

5

rit.

2. Sightread each example when you have finished writing the left-hand part.

54

The C Chord

The C chord is made of 3 notes
that build up in 3rds from C.

- C is the **root** - E is the **3rd** - G is the **5th**

The C chord is called the I chord
(pronounced "one") in the C Pentascale.

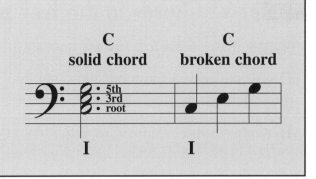

This folk song is composed only of **C chord notes**.
Answer the Study Questions below before playing.

English Folk Song
(Study Piece)

Traditional

A Closer Look at English Folk Song

(Study Questions)

1. a. In each blank write **solid** or **broken** to describe the chord.

   b. Write the 3 letter names used in this piece. ____, ____, ____

   c. In which three bars does the R.H. melody begin

      on the **3rd** of the chord? *bars* ____, ____, ____

   d. Draw a **semibreve rest** to complete each empty bar.

2. Now sightread *English Folk Song*.

Lessons p. 78

I and V⁷ Chords in the Key of C

V is the Roman numeral for the number 5.

The **V⁷ chord** is a four-note chord built up in 3rds from the **dominant** (scale degree 5).

The notes of the **V⁷ chord** are often rearranged to form a three-note chord. (See Lesson Book, page 82.)

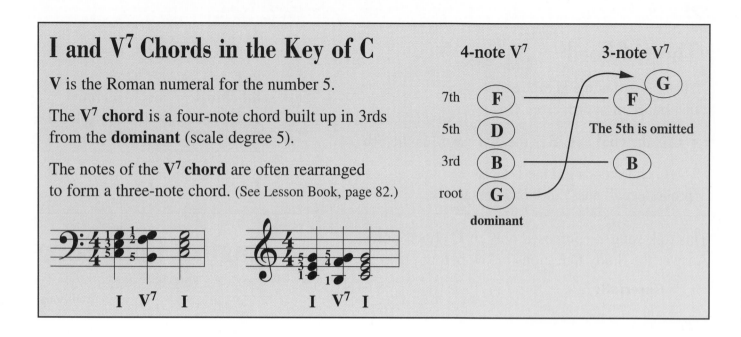

In popular music, the "lead" (pronounced "LEED") means the melody.

A *lead sheet* is the melody *only*, with **chord symbols** written above the stave.

● First play the melody only.

● Then add **solid I** and **V⁷ chords** in the left hand as indicated by the chord symbols.

Jingle Bells

(A First Lead Sheet)

First sightread the melodies.

Then add **I** and **V⁷ chords** in the left hand as indicated by the **chord symbols.**

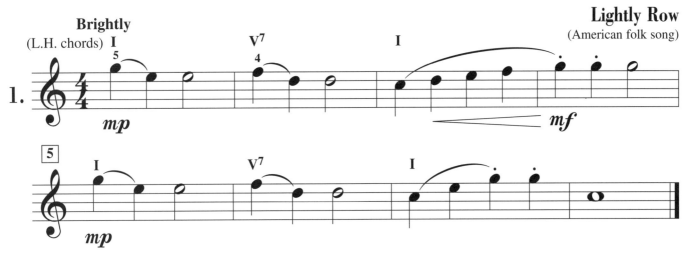

Lightly Row
(American folk song)

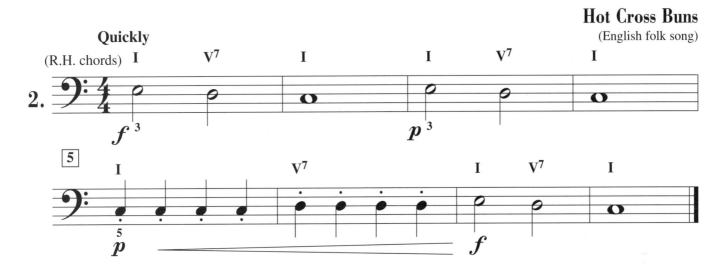

Hot Cross Buns
(English folk song)

1. Place your L.H. in the Bass C Position.

2. Close your eyes as your teacher plays a short example using **I** and **V⁷** chords. *Listen* carefully.

3. Play back what you hear.

Note: If two pianos are available, the teacher and student can each play in the same octave.

For Teacher Use Only: (The teacher may play the examples in any order and repeat as often as necessary.)

It is recommended that the teacher continue this ear training exercise at future lessons, using other combinations of I and V⁷ chords.

UNIT 12

Three G Positions

1. Name each note in the blank for the **G Positions** below.

2. Write each **G Pentascale** on the staves below. Use semibreves.

Then shade the *tonic* and *dominant* notes.

Treble Clef G Position

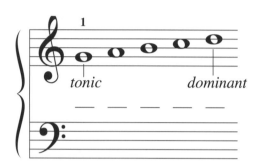

Treble Clef G Pentascale

Bass Clef G Position

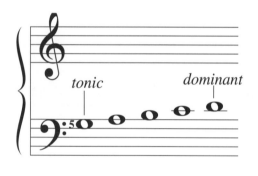

Bass Clef G Pentascale

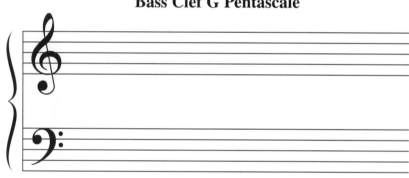

Low G Position

Low G Pentascale

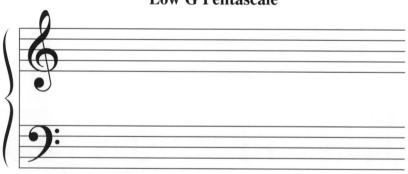

3. Put stems on all the G Pentascale notes you have written.

Remember: For notes **on** or **above line 3**, use *down* stems (on the left side).

For notes **below line 3**, use *up* stems (on the right side).

(See page 42.)

Seven Guide Notes

1. Name these seven Guide Notes.

• Write and name these seven Guide Notes from *lowest* to *highest*.

• Write and name these seven Guide Notes from *highest* to *lowest*.

Guide Note Strategy

2. Draw the *closest* Guide Note to the left of each note shown. Then name both notes in the blanks.

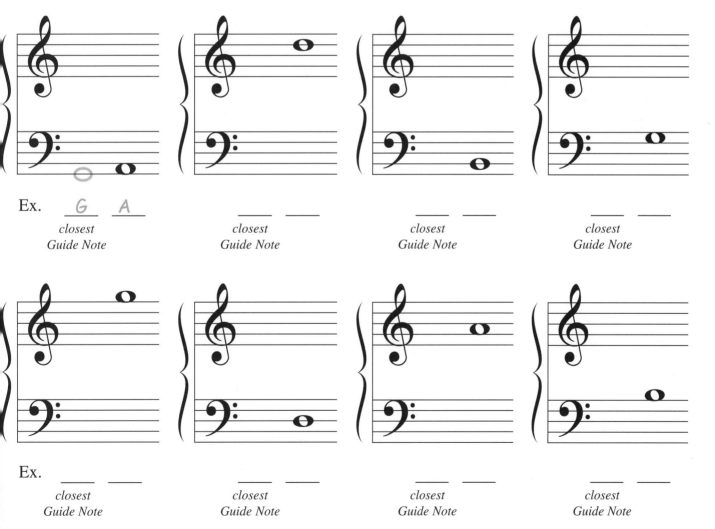

Ex. G   A
   closest
   Guide Note

____ ____
   closest
   Guide Note

____ ____
   closest
   Guide Note

____ ____
   closest
   Guide Note

Ex. ____ ____
   closest
   Guide Note

____ ____
   closest
   Guide Note

____ ____
   closest
   Guide Note

____ ____
   closest
   Guide Note

3. Play each example above on the keyboard.

Lessons p. 87

Treble G Position

Treble G   A   B   C   D

Composing Your Own Musette

Compose your own *musette** in **G Position**.

- Use the rhythm given above the stave for the **R.H.** melody.
- Create your melody from the Treble G Position notes (shown above).
- Play slowly, hands together. Then play at a lively tempo.

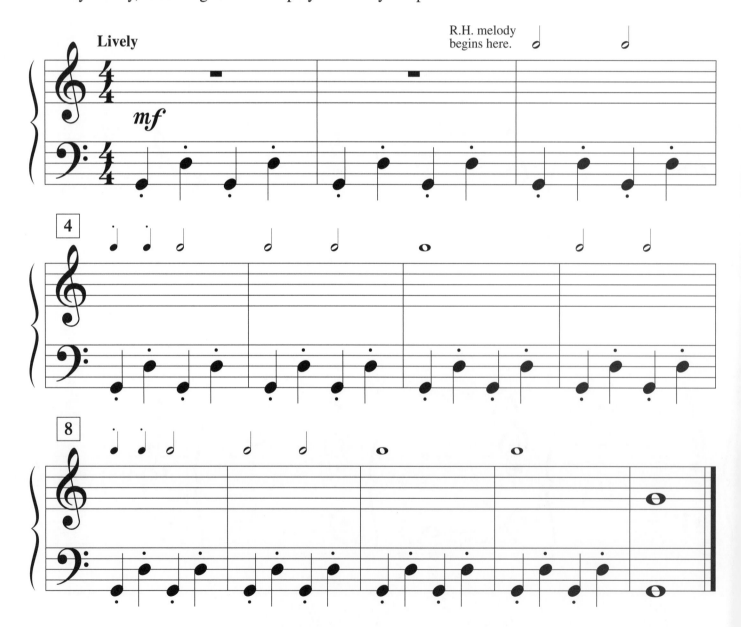

*A *musette* is a lively piece that imitates the sound of a bagpipe.

I and V⁷ Chords in the Key of G

I   V⁷   I   I   V⁷   I

Review: A *gavotte* is a lively French dance in $\frac{4}{4}$ time. It usually begins with two upbeats.

Remember, a *lead sheet* is the melody only with *chord symbols* written above the stave.

1. First play the melody only.

Then add **solid I** and **V⁷ chords** in the **key of G** as indicated by the chord symbols.

Gavotte

(Lead Sheet in G Major)

George Frideric Handel
(1685–1759, Germany)

2. Play *high* on the keyboard with the teacher duet.

Teacher Duet: (Student plays *high* on the keyboard)

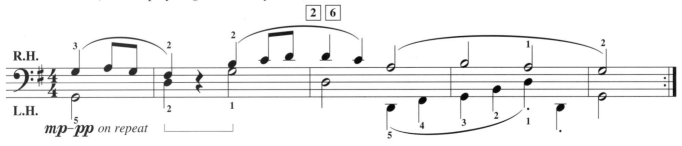

Lessons p. 90

Rhythm Workout

(Review of I and V⁷ chords
in the Key of G)

1. Write the counts **1 + 2 +** (for *"1 and 2 and"*) for this $\frac{2}{4}$ rhythm.
Then play, counting aloud.

Count: 1   +   2   +

(you write)

2. Write the counts **1 + 2 + 3 +** for this $\frac{3}{4}$ rhythm.
Then play, counting aloud.

Count: 1   +

(you write)

3. Write the counts **1 + 2 + 3 + 4 +** for this $\frac{4}{4}$ rhythm.
Then play, counting aloud.

Count: 1   +   *(you write)*

4. Write four bars of your own $\frac{4}{4}$ rhythm below.
Then write **I** or **V⁷** in each box.
Play your rhythm using the chords you have chosen.

chord
symbol:

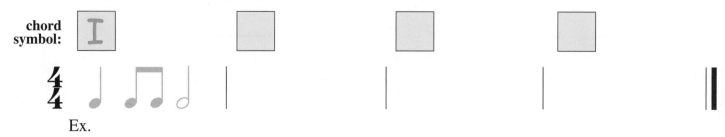

Ex.

- Sightread these **G major** melodies.

- Then add *harmony* (see Lesson Book, page 82) by writing **I** or **V⁷** in the boxes. *Listen* and let your ears guide you.

- Play each melody with the chords. (Remember the *F-sharp* in the **V⁷** chord.)

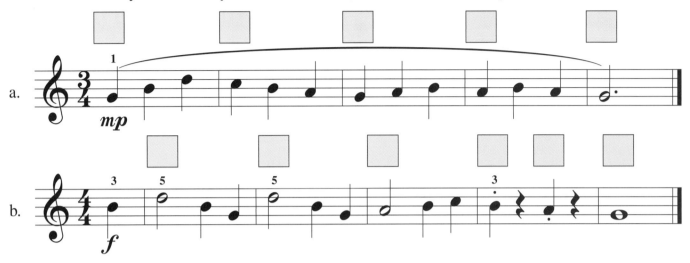

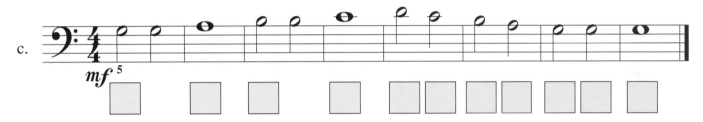

Your teacher will play a short example that will end on the **I** or **V⁷** chord. Circle the correct answer for the last chord.

Hint: The **I** chord sounds *restful* and **complete**.
The **V⁷** chord sounds *restless* and **incomplete**.

1. **I**	2. **I**	3. **I**	4. **I**
or	or	or	or
V⁷	**V⁷**	**V⁷**	**V⁷**

For Teacher Use Only: (The examples may be played in any order.)

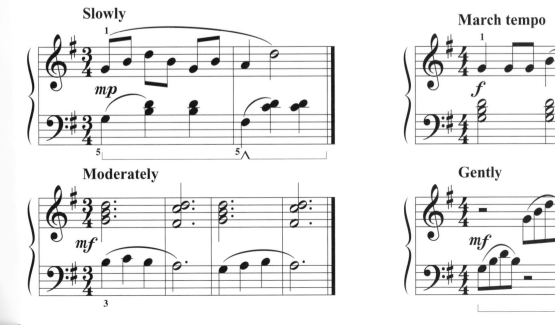

Final Review

Musical Terms Crossword Puzzle

Complete this crossword puzzle and review 18 musical terms!

The answers are given upside down at the bottom of the page.

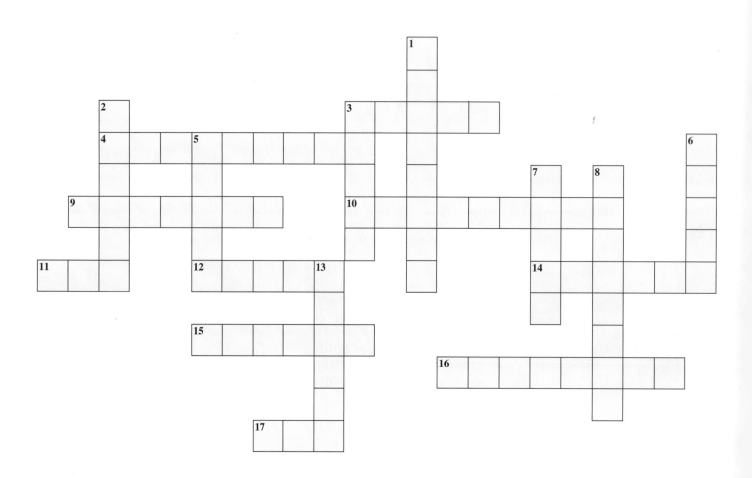

Across

3. Scale degree 1 of the C Pentascale.
4. Play gradually louder.
9. Hold this note longer than usual.
10. A musical passage echoed by the other hand.
11. Abbreviation for the term that means a gradual slowing of the tempo.
12. Play softly.
14. Another name for the G clef.
15. The interval that spans four letter names.
16. Scale degree 5 of the scale.
17. A curved line that connects one note to the very same note.

Down

1. The "louds and softs" of music.
2. Play this note louder.
3. Scale degree 1 of the G Pentascale.
5. Raises the note a semitone.
6. Play loudly.
7. The interval that spans five letter names.
8. The distance between two pitches (notes) or keys on the keyboard.
13. The interval that spans 8 letter names.